A IS FOR AIR

The Wright Brothers invented flight.
Michael "Air" Jordan perfected it.

B IS FOR BIRD

The legendary Larry Bird chirped with the best of them, but he had the game to back it up.

C IS FOR COOKING

If you can't stand the heat, stay out of the kitchen – the Beard is cooking.

D IS FOR DOCTOR

His game was clinical.
His operating room an arena.
The one and only Dr. J.

E IS FOR EURO

One-legged fadeaway, all day.
German Dirk Nowitzki was Europe's
finest export.

F IS FOR **FAST BREAK**

Two-time MVP Steve Nash could burn your
defense in seven seconds or less.

G IS FOR GRANDMAMA

Sorry Madea, "Grandmama" Larry Johnson is the
real G-GOAT – the Greatest Grandma of All Time.

H IS FOR HUGE HUMAN HURTING HOOPS

Bring it down, big fella, bring it down. Shaq's super strength left a pile of broken backboards in his path.

I IS FOR ICEMAN

Ice be cool. "The Iceman" George Gervin finger-rolled his way onto nine All-Star teams without breaking a sweat.

J IS FOR JAM

Jam on. When Bill Walton wasn't jamming on the court, he was jamming with the Grateful Dead.

K IS FOR KING

Pass, board, score or defend. They call him
the King because LeBron can do it all.

L IS FOR LITTLE

Just 5-foot-3, little Muggsy Bogues lasted fourteen seasons in the land of giants.

M IS FOR MAILMAN

High on the mountain top, a postman's on patrol. Watch out – when Karl sets a pick, it's hard to slow the roll.

N IS FOR NINETIES

What a time to be alive.

MULLIN

EWING

THE ADMIRAL

DIKEMBE

THE DREAM

THE GLOVE   REIGN MAN   STOCKTON   PIP   SIR CHARLES

O IS FOR ONE HUNDRED

Only one man ever scored one hundred points in one game: Wilt Chamberlain.

P IS FOR PISTOL

"Pistol" Pete averaged 44 points a game in college. If they had threes back then, he'd have averaged over 50.

Q IS FOR QUESTION

And the ANSWER is ALLEN IVERSON
— 165 pounds of pure heart.

R IS FOR RINGS

Quiet and consistent, Tim Duncan knew a thing or ~~two~~ five about winning: It don't mean a thing without that ring.

KAREEM

BIG GAME JAMES

S IS FOR SHOWTIME

Pull up a seat. Enjoy the show. Magic and crew are putting on a performance.

T IS FOR THREES

Layups are nice and dunks are dope,
but threes are better 'cause they're worth the most.

U IS FOR UNCLE

Listen up, youngbloods: Uncle Drew and his buddy Bill Russell need you to understand that this game has always been, and will always be, about buckets.

V IS FOR VENOM

Beware. Kobe was known to strike like the venomous
Black Mamba – the fastest, most feared snake in the world.

W IS FOR WORM

Wriggling, wrestling and worming for every board, Dennis Rodman wasn't afraid to do the dirty work down low.

X IS FOR X'S AND O'S

They know their X's. They know their O's. Coaches change the game without ever touching the rock.

Y IS FOR YOU THE REAL MVP

His arms are slender. His heart is tender. It doesn't matter what he says, KD is the real MVP.

Z IS FOR ZERO

Russell Westbrook wears number zero — the same number of players who look forward to facing him.

THE END is just the beginning...